# Mothering Sunday

A play

Olwen Wymark

Samuel French—London
New York-Toronto-Hollywood

© 2002 BY OLWEN WYMARK

Rights of Performance by Amateurs are controlled by Samuel French Ltd, 52 Fitzroy Street, London W1T 5JR, and they, or their authorized agents, issue licences to amateurs on payment of a fee. **It is an infringement of the Copyright to give any performance or public reading of the play before the fee has been paid and the licence issued.**

The Royalty Fee indicated below is subject to contract and subject to variation at the sole discretion of Samuel French Ltd.

    Basic fee for each and every
      performance by amateurs    Code E
      in the British Isles

The Professional Rights in this play are controlled by THE AGENCY (LONDON) LTD, 24 Pottery Lane, Holland Park, London W11 4LZ.

**The publication of this play does not imply that it is necessarily available for performance by amateurs or professionals, either in the British Isles or Overseas. Amateurs and professionals considering a production are strongly advised in their own interests to apply to the appropriate agents for written consent before starting rehearsals or booking a theatre or hall.**

ISBN 0 573 02354 9

Please see page iv for further copyright information

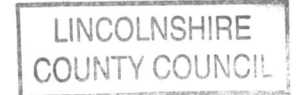

LINCOLNSHIRE
COUNTY COUNCIL

## CHARACTERS

**Geraldine**: very attractive, a little overweight; intelligent, warm, witty and domineering; 41

**Doug**: very good-looking boxer, sweet-natured and loyal; 32

**Sidney**: Geraldine's daughter. Student. Very bright, very pretty, rather domineering like her mother; 19

**Alex**: journalist; laid back, very clever, very selfish; 36

The action of the play takes place in the living-room of Geraldine's cottage in Surrey

Time—the present

## COPYRIGHT INFORMATION
(See also page ii)

This play is fully protected under the Copyright Laws of the British Commonwealth of Nations, the United States of America and all countries of the Berne and Universal Copyright Conventions.

All rights, including Stage, Motion Picture, Radio, Television, Public Reading, and Translation into Foreign Languages, are strictly reserved.

**No part of this publication may lawfully be reproduced in ANY form or by any means — photocopying, typescript, recording (including video-recording), manuscript, electronic, mechanical, or otherwise — or be transmitted or stored in a retrieval system, without prior permission.**

Licences are issued subject to the understanding that it shall be made clear in all advertising matter that the audience will witness an amateur performance; that the names of the authors of the plays shall be included on all announcements and on all programmes; and that the integrity of the authors' work will be preserved.

The Royalty Fee is subject to contract and subject to variation at the sole discretion of Samuel French Ltd.

In Theatres or Halls seating Four Hundred or more the fee will be subject to negotiation.

In Territories Overseas the fee quoted in this Acting Edition may not apply. A fee will be quoted on application to our local authorized agent, or if there is no such agent, on application to Samuel French Ltd, London.

---

### VIDEO-RECORDING OF AMATEUR PRODUCTIONS

Please note that the copyright laws governing video-recording are extremely complex and that it should not be assumed that any play may be video-recorded for *whatever purpose* without first obtaining the permission of the appropriate agents. The fact that a play is published by Samuel French Ltd does not indicate that video rights are available or that Samuel French Ltd controls such rights.

*Other plays by Olwen Wymark published by
Samuel French Ltd*

Brezhnev's Children
Find Me
Lessons and Lovers
Loved
Strike Up the Banns

# MOTHERING SUNDAY

*The living-room of Geraldine's cottage in Surrey*

*There are three doors; one* UL *is the front door, one* UR *leads to a bedroom, one* DR *leads to the kitchen. There is one small window. The room is rather bare but very elegantly decorated. There is a low antique chest* US *with an abstract painting hanging over it. In the room are a modern sofa, a coffee table, a couple of good chairs, a bookshelf with books, an expensive oriental rug, a baby grand piano with stool and sheet music, and a sports bag*

*When the play begins the stage is in darkness. Music plays. This cross-fades to the sound of a a simple piece being played on the piano, not very well*

*The Lights come up. At the piano are Geraldine and Doug. She's wearing a chic track suit and is barefoot. Doug is in jeans and T-shirt*

**Geraldine** And two and three and four and one and two and ——

*Doug hits a wrong note and stops playing, looking depressed*

Never mind. Take it from the top. Cheer up, Doug. It's coming along fine.

**Doug** You said we were going to bed.

**Geraldine** After your piano practice.

**Doug** I'll never be able to play this flaming piece.

**Geraldine** Now, Doug, don't be such a defeatist. Of course you will.

**Doug** Gerry, I've been practising it for months. You have to learn piano playing when you're a little kid. Thirty-two's too old.

**Geraldine** No, it isn't. Come along. Once more.

*Doug puts his hands on the wrong keys, plays, then stops, amazed*

**Doug** What happened?
**Geraldine** You've got your fingers in the wrong place, dummy.
**Doug** It's no use. I got the wrong kind of hands altogether is the thing. Boxers can't play the piano.
**Geraldine** Anyone can play the piano. It just takes concentration.
**Doug** Oh, Gerry, can't we just go to bed now? She'll be here soon.
**Geraldine** Don't be silly. Half past three at the earliest.
**Doug** Well it's nearly one o'clock now!
**Geraldine** Twelve-fifteen. If you won't do your piano practice we'll get on with the poetry.
**Doug** Proper tease you are, Gerry.
**Geraldine** (*punching Doug's back*) I am not.
**Doug** Ooch. (*Admiringly*) You're getting very good at that kidney punch, you know that?
**Geraldine** Thank you. Take back what you said or I'll do it again. Harder. (*She aims another punch*)

*Doug laughs, grabs Geraldine's arm and puts it behind her back*

Ow. Stop. That's not fair. You're stronger than me. Stop! You're breaking my arm.
**Doug** (*letting go*) Sorry, Gerry. Didn't mean to really hurt you. You OK?
**Geraldine** Yes. Now. I am not a tease. Am I?
**Doug** No, you're not.
**Geraldine** I am simply trying to open the doors of art and literature and music to you. You're like a deprived child.
**Doug** I'm not a child.
**Geraldine** You are to me.
**Doug** Nine years older doesn't make me a child. Anyway if you think that ... (*He kisses her neck*)
**Geraldine** Stop that. I told you. After your poetry lesson. Douglas! I mean it.

# Mothering Sunday

**Doug** OK. Give us a kiss, then. Come on. Just one.
**Geraldine** Oh all right.

*They kiss*

> (*Breathlessly*) That's enough. (*She breaks away and goes to the bookshelf*)

*Doug follows Geraldine, puts his arms round her and kisses her again*

**Geraldine** (*beaming at Doug*) You're a sex maniac.
**Doug** No, I just fancy you like mad.
**Geraldine** Now sit down, Douglas. (*She takes a book from the shelf and finds a page in it*) Here's the page. Well there's no need to look so tragic. (*Pause*) Perhaps you'd rather read to me in bed.
**Doug** Would I!

*Doug jumps up and leads Geraldine towards the door* UR. *She stops*

**Geraldine** No, wait. We'd better do the room first.

*Doug groans*

> Then it's done. It'll only take five minutes. (*She kisses him*) Come on.

*During the following dialogue, Geraldine goes to the chest and takes out a lot of flowered cushions, antimacassars, a big fringed satin shawl and a lacy table runner. She drapes the shawl over the piano and puts the table runner on the coffee table. As she does so, Doug puts the cushions on the sofa and the antimacassars on the chairs. They take framed photographs, china ornaments etc. out of the chest and put them on the piano and the coffee table*

**Doug** There'd be plenty of time for art and music and that if I was just living here.

**Geraldine** You can't. It would upset Sidney.
**Doug** Really weird name for a girl. No wonder she's so peculiar.
**Geraldine** She's not peculiar. She's just going through a phase. It's only a year since the divorce and she's got enough to cope with, with him getting married again. (*Beat*) To that idiot.
**Doug** I can see why you told her I was the plumber when she saw me that time, you not wanting her to know about us having a ding-dong but ——
**Geraldine** (*pained*) Ding-dong?
**Doug** Well, we are. But you got to admit she doesn't look like the kind of girl that could be upset by anything.
**Geraldine** I'm sure she'll grow out of all that. She's only nineteen. I think myself it was a reaction to that stuck up finishing school in Switzerland. I hated her going there but he insisted. He is such a snob.
**Doug** Well, all this still seems daft to me. Changing everything around. (*He rolls up the rug, puts it into the chest and takes another one out — a very bright Spanish rug*)
**Geraldine** I'm trying to win her back, Doug. She's been completely off me since the divorce.
**Doug** I think she'd like you better the way you really are.

*They roll out the Spanish rug together*

**Geraldine** I have to convince her that I'm not a fallen woman.
**Doug** (*indignantly*) You're not,
**Geraldine** Of course I'm not, but he's turned her against me. He told her a lot of lies about how the divorce was all my fault. Which it bloody wasn't.

*Doug moves to take the painting down; Geraldine follows and helps him. Together they put up a gaudy pastoral sunset scene*

As if anyone could compete with him in the infidelity stakes. It makes me so furious that he probably told her I was having an affair.
**Doug** But you weren't.

# Mothering Sunday

**Geraldine** (*promptly*) No, I wasn't.

**Doug** So why not tell her it was a lie.

**Geraldine** Well, because ... Because (*fluently*) she's actually very fond of him and I don't believe in coming between parent and child.

**Doug** Right. But he came between her and you.

**Geraldine** (*sadly*) Yes. Anyway, now she's agreed to come and see me every Sunday, I have to show her that I'm just a nice ordinary motherly person who is not obsessed with sex.

**Doug** (*moving towards her*) You sure?

**Geraldine** (*dodging him, laughing*) Doug ... (*She takes a pair of bronzed baby shoes out of the chest and hands them to him*)

**Geraldine** On the piano.

**Doug** This is new. These her shoes when she was a kiddie?

**Geraldine** No, I got them at a jumble sale. Well, I think that's it.

*Doug puts his arms round Geraldine*

Oh. The knitting. Did you do some more?

**Doug** Yep. Quite a bit. (*He moves to his sports bag and takes out a long scarf on knitting needles*)

**Geraldine** Perfect. I really should learn myself. (*She takes the knitting from Doug and puts it on the sofa*) I don't deserve you, Doug.

**Doug** Don't talk silly. I'm the lucky one. I never know what you see in me.

**Geraldine** (*laughing*) That's what.

**Doug** What?

**Geraldine** That you don't see what I see in you.

**Doug** (*baffled*) Right.

**Geraldine** (*hugging him*) And because you're the only truly nice sweet man I ever met in my life. Do you think you could knit a cardigan?

**Doug** (*worriedly*) Oh, well, blimey — I don't know. I never knitted anything big. But I'll have a go.

**Geraldine** Thank you. Then I could give it to Sidney. A fallen woman wouldn't knit a cardigan. (*Pause*) Probably wouldn't help. (*Sadly*) Sometimes I think she actually hates me.

**Doug** She couldn't. Nobody could. (*Upset*) Don't be upset, Gerry. (*He puts his arms round her*) You're perfect. I love you, you know that, don't you? You're the only woman I ever met I can talk to. It's like you're really interested in me personally. What I think and all that. I mean it's not just the sex. (*Beat*) But maybe we could go to bed now, eh?
**Geraldine** (*kissing Doug*) Maybe we could.

*Doug takes Geraldine's hand and leads her to the door* UR

*The Lights fade to Black-out*

*Music plays; this cross-fades to the distant sound of church bells striking three, then the sound of a car pulling up outside with screeching brakes. A car door opens and shuts*

*The Lights slowly come up*

**Sidney** (*off*) Are you coming or not?
**Alex** (*off*) Give me a second to recover, all right? Jesus, Sidney, you're a terrible driver.
**Sidney** (*off*) I am not. I used to drive my father all the time.
**Alex** (*off*) I don't remember him being a masochist.
**Sidney** (*off*) You told me you never even met him.

*There is the sound of a door knocker*

**Alex** (*off*) I knew people that knew him.
**Geraldine** (*off; as if from upstairs*) Oh, my God! She's here! Doug! Wake up!
**Sidney** (*off*) How funny. She usually answers right away. (*She mimics Geraldine*) Sidney — darling!
**Alex** (*off*) So maybe she's gone out.
**Sidney** (*off*) She'd never go out on Sunday. It's a really big thing for her me coming. She bakes a cake and everything.

*The door knocker sounds again*

Mothering Sunday

*Doug enters* UR. *He is barefoot and wearing just his trousers, which he zips up as he enters. He heads across the room at speed*

**Geraldine** (*off, in an urgent whisper*) Get down! The window!

*Doug adopts a crouch and runs to the door* UR

*Geraldine appears* UR *in a short silk dressing-gown, holding Doug's shoes and shirt*

**Geraldine** (*in a loud whisper*) Doug!

*Doug turns. Geraldine holds up his things. The knocker sounds again*

**Sidney** (*off*) Where is she?

*Doug and Geraldine freeze. Then, both crouching, they run towards each other. He grabs the shoes and shirt and kisses her on the lips*

**Geraldine** (*in a frenzied whisper*) Go! Go!

*Doug gets his sports bag and crouch-runs out* DR

*Geraldine crouch-runs towards the door* UR

**Alex** (*off*) The door's unlocked.
**Sidney** (*off*) Well we can't just walk in.
**Alex** (*off*) Why not?

*Geraldine achieves the* UR *door with a frantic leap; she exits, shutting the door behind her*

*Alex strolls in* UL, *followed by Sidney. She is wearing Doc Martens and a black mini-dress and has her hair in spikes*

**Sidney** She won't like it. She's very conventional.

**Alex** Conventional? Your mother was always ... Dear God! (*He stops dead and stares around the room*)

**Sidney** What?

**Alex** This room! She can't possibly live with all this — stuff! She's not like this.

**Sidney** Why do you say that? You only met her once.

**Alex** (*promptly*) Right.

**Sidney** My father says she's always been basically dowdy.

**Alex** Dowdy? I thought she was quite glamorous.

**Sidney** I did too, once. And she was really, you know, witty. Or I thought she was. Now I know that was all just a front. (*She gestures at the room*) This is the real her. God! A cottage in Surrey! Dad says she's simply reverted to type since the divorce. Like a psychological regression.

**Alex** Really. Well, nobody could accuse you of being dowdy. This is what they're wearing in smart Kensington these days?

**Sidney** I only dress like this because she expects it. I told her I went punk in Switzerland. I knew she'd hate that. It was a way of getting back at her for sending me there. My father tried to stop her but she insisted. Because she wanted me out of the way on account of feeling guilty about breaking up their marriage.

**Alex** Wait a minute. He started it. She didn't play around at all till after she found out he ... (*He breaks off*) Well, that's what people said.

**Sidney** (*staring*) Play around?

**Alex** You know. Affairs. That was the gossip.

**Sidney** She never had any affairs.

**Alex** Oh. Right.

**Sidney** Quite the reverse, actually. She literally drove my father into adultery because she was totally frigid. She's one of those women who's afraid of sex.

**Alex** Sorry?

**Sidney** It's quite common in that age group. But it was a real tragedy for him. He was forced into celibacy for years. He only stayed for my sake. He told me about it after the divorce.

**Alex** I see.

**Sidney** I wonder where she is. I have to get back and finish an English Lit. paper for tomorrow.

**Alex** On what?

**Sidney** A study of primal subtextual emotional interplay in Jane Austen through the use of mirrors and reflections.

**Alex** Dear heaven.

**Sidney** Maybe she's out in the garden.

**Alex** Shall I go and have a look?

**Sidney** Yes, do. That way. Through the kitchen.

*Alex goes out* DR

*Sidney picks up ornaments and puts them down, shaking her head*

*Geraldine appears through the* UR *door. She's slightly breathless and wearing a tweed skirt that's a bit too tight with a cashmere twin set and pearls. She takes a deep breath*

**Geraldine** (*tugging down her girdle; enthusiastically*) Sidney — darling!

**Sidney** (*with a pronounced cockney accent*) Hallo. Thought you'd gone out or something.

**Geraldine** On a Sunday? No, I didn't hear you arrive. I was — er — turning out the linen cupboard.

**Sidney** Brought a friend this time. OK?

**Geraldine** Goodness yes, of course. How lovely. Where is she?

**Sidney** It's a him. He says he met you once at a party a long time ago.

*Alex enters and smiles at Geraldine*

Oh. Right on cue! Alex, meet my mum.

*Geraldine stands stock still, staring at Alex*

**Alex** (*very friendly*) I expect you've forgotten me.

**Geraldine** (*very unfriendly*) No. (*Pause. In a social manner*) Have you and Sidney known each other long?

**Sidney** Only a week. He picked me up in a pub in Mile End. Round the corner from the place I'm squatting.

**Geraldine** (*upset*) Squatting? I thought your father was going to buy you a flat.

**Sidney** I told him I didn't want it. (*Scornfully*) Kensington? Talk about uncool! (*She moves to the piano and picks out Doug's piece with one finger during the following*)

**Alex** Very quaint little place you have here.

**Geraldine** (*graciously*) So glad you like it.

**Alex** Somehow it's not quite what I would have pictured you in. From the old days.

**Geraldine** Really? There have been so many changes in my life, Mr … I'm sorry, I can't remember your name.

**Alex** Oh, please. Call me Alex. And I'll call you Geraldine, shall I?

**Geraldine** (*too cordially*) Do!

*Sidney sits down at the piano and plays the piece all the way through. Well. Alex applauds*

**Sidney** I used to play that piece, didn't I?

*Geraldine smiles at Sidney and Sidney nearly smiles back, but stops herself*

**Geraldine** Yes, you did. Have you started your lessons again?

**Sidney** (*unpleasantly*) You kidding? No chance.

**Geraldine** You haven't changed your mind about going to university?

**Sidney** Bloody waste of time.

**Alex** But you ——

**Sidney** University's useless, Alex. I told you that.

**Alex** So you did. (*He picks up the bronze shoes*) What are these?

**Geraldine** Sidney's very first shoes. From when she was a kiddie.

**Sidney** Jesus wept!

**Alex** And is this your knitting, Geraldine?

**Geraldine** (*snapping*) Yes it is. (*Cordial again*) I always knit while I'm listening to the wireless. Have you heard from your father, Sidney?

**Sidney** Yeah. He wants me to go out to LA and live with them.

**Geraldine** (*alarmed*) Are you going to?

**Sidney** God no, I can't stand her.

**Geraldine** (*pleased*) Really?

**Sidney** She's a cow.

**Geraldine** (*beaming*) I'm sure she isn't.

**Sidney** She is. And stupid. Anyway I don't want to go to LA now I'm living with Alex, do I?

*Geraldine stops smiling*

**Sidney** You OK, Mum?

**Geraldine** (*breathlessly*) Fine. I must go and get the tea.

*Geraldine exits quickly into the kitchen* DR, *closing the door behind her*

**Sidney** (*not cockney*) That got her. She was really shocked.

**Alex** Sidney, you don't want us to live together, do you?

**Sidney** Good heavens, no. I'm really too busy for relationships.

**Alex** Impetuous hotheaded romantic youth. Nothing like it.

**Sidney** I honestly think romance is outdated. After all, with efficient contraception there's no need for all that pretence. Sex is just a physiological need.

**Alex** Oh. Right.

**Sidney** When you're hungry you eat, when you're tired you sleep and when you need ——

**Alex** I don't believe it! I used to say those exact same words to girls I wanted to get into bed when I was your age.

**Sidney** (*kindly*) The whirligig of time. I usually go for a walk before tea. Want to come?

**Alex** No thanks. I hate walking in the country.
**Sidney** Poor you. I love it. (*She heads for the front door*) Back soon.
**Alex** Tally ho.
**Sidney** (*calling*) Mum? Just going out to smoke some dope.

*Sidney exits*

*As the door closes behind Sidney, Geraldine appears through the door* DR

**Geraldine** Sidney, what did you ——?
**Alex** Hallo, Gerry.
**Geraldine** Don't speak to me, you monster! How could you?
**Alex** How could I what?
**Geraldine** She's only a child! And besides, it's like incest!
**Alex** (*pleased*) You're jealous.
**Geraldine** I am not. I'm morally outraged.
**Alex** How could it be incest? I'm not related to either of you.
**Geraldine** No, but we're related to each other. And you're old enough to be her father.
**Alex** I'm bloody not. He's forty-eight.
**Geraldine** How even you could do such a ——
**Alex** Such a what? I got back from Argentina last week. I tried to find you. Couldn't. Tracked down Sidney. Told her I'd met you once in the dear old days. Then last night she told me she was going to visit you today so it seemed quite a jolly idea to spend the night with her and drive her down here to have tea with you today.
**Geraldine** Jolly! Cold-blooded revenge, that's what it was, wasn't it. Revenge.
**Alex** (*affable*) Yes, I expect it was.
**Geraldine** How absolutely vile and horrible and disgusting. And childish. And typical. You don't love her, do you?
**Alex** Certainly not. Do you?
**Geraldine** Of course I do. Naturally. She's my daughter.
**Alex** Oh yes. Naturally. Of course.
**Geraldine** Stop being suave and cynical. I do love her and it's my job to protect her from people like you.

Mothering Sunday

**Alex** Sidney doesn't need protection. She regards me as an academic exercise. The older stud.

**Geraldine** Don't be so revolting. I always knew you were selfish and unscrupulous but how you could use Sidney like ——

**Alex** (*stung*) And who used me? Who was the rejected unhappy wife who needed her sexual morale bolstering up? Oh, not by one of her smart intellectual artistic friends. No, no, just a boring tabloid journalist who happened to be good in bed.

**Geraldine** Alex, stop.

*At some point during the following speech, Geraldine laughs*

**Alex** I won't stop. Why the hell should I? You bloody well ruined my life. You knew you were the only woman I'd ever really loved. You liked that of course, but marry me? There was never any question of that in your mind and you didn't give a damn what was in mine. So I was left without anybody or anything. Desperate, suicidal, absolutely alone and — why are you laughing?

**Geraldine** Oh, Alex, you haven't changed a bit. You're such a bastard.

**Alex** What's that supposed to mean?

**Geraldine** Don't you remember phoning me at four o'clock in the morning — when was it? About two years ago.

**Alex** I really don't know what ——

**Geraldine** I hadn't seen you for weeks and there you were saying would I marry you and when I said I wouldn't, you said you'd kill yourself. (*Pause*) I cried! You said you were desperate and suicidal and absolutely alone — and you'd been living with that Chinese movie starlet for a month.

**Alex** (*interestedly*) How did you find that out?

**Geraldine** (*coldly*) People told me things.

**Alex** She was an awful girl.

**Geraldine** That's as may be. I was the one who was absolutely alone.

**Alex** But not any more, I gather.

**Geraldine** I don't know what you're talking about. What makes you think that?

**Alex** People tell me things. And do you really think you can fool me with (*he gestures at the room*) all this? Maybe your kooky daughter can believe in you as a cosy country lady but not me. I suppose you're president of the local Women's Institute.

**Geraldine** Treasurer. How was Buenos Aires?

**Alex** Terrific.

**Geraldine** Why didn't you stay there?

**Alex** Conveniently out from under your feet, you mean. You're the one who hasn't changed. Still in charge, still wanting everybody to dance to your tune.

**Geraldine** Oh, don't be so boring.

**Alex** Would it be less boring if I told your little girl what chums you and I used to be?

**Geraldine** You wouldn't!

**Alex** I might. So who are you chums with nowadays, Gerry?

**Geraldine** I have no idea what you mean.

**Alex** Someone mentioned a wrestler. Or was it a boxer?

**Geraldine** Oh really, can't you see I don't lead that kind of life?

**Alex** What I see is someone who used to be an elegant and rather dangerous woman masquerading as a tea cosy. Look at all this. Photos of the Royal Family? Antimacassars? Knitting, for Christ's sake? This room is like some kind of stage set!

**Geraldine** What a silly thing to say. This is my home! Sidney's been talking to you about me, hasn't she. Her father telling her I'm some kind of heartless nymphomaniac ——

**Alex** What? No, she ——

**Geraldine** (*overriding*) And that's what you think too, isn't it. That I'm a selfish, depraved woman who ——

**Alex** Actually it was more ——

**Geraldine** (*just going on*) Impossible that I could be living a simple quiet life in the country … Oh of course!

**Alex** Gerry, you ——

**Geraldine** So you set about seducing my daughter, tracking me down, blackmailing me ——

**Alex** (*laughing*) Blackmail!

**Geraldine** Well, why are you here?

**Alex** I wanted to find out if it was true about the wrestler.

Mothering Sunday

**Geraldine** (*furiously*) Fine! Where is he then? Would you like to search the house? Go ahead! Go on!

**Alex** Gerry, there's no need to get in a state.

**Geraldine** Yes there is. I'm very upset. (*Poignantly*) You of all people, Alex. I thought you cared for me. After you left me, all I wanted was peace and solitude and ——

**Alex** Wait a minute. You left me!

**Geraldine** Not at all. You went to Argentina.

**Alex** Because you wouldn't marry me!

**Geraldine** Oh Alex, you never really wanted to marry me.

**Alex** I bloody did.

**Geraldine** (*kindly*) No, no. You thought you did but you didn't really.

**Alex** Talk about typical. You're always doing this — telling people what they want, what they feel, what they think. You're so bloody bossy!

**Geraldine** I am not bossy!

**Alex** Yes, you are. You're like a beautiful bully of a sergeant major.

**Geraldine** (*after a pause; sweetly*) Poor Alex.

**Alex** (*warily*) What do you mean, poor?

**Geraldine** You just can't understand that I've made a new life for myself out here. Pottering about in the garden, playing my piano, yes knitting too. And all my committee work, of course.

**Alex** (*bemusedly*) Committee?

**Geraldine** I told you I'm treasurer of the WI. It means a lot to me, believe me. It was such a thrill the day Jojo appointed me.

**Alex** Jojo?

**Geraldine** Her name's really Josephine but we all call her Jojo. She's chairperson and she's my dearest friend in the village. She's an amazing woman. And so artistic. She's started all of us on watercolouring and we have our writers' circle at her house once a week. My life is so full now. So rewarding and ——

**Alex** (*shaken*) Stop, Gerry, just stop. None of this is true.

**Geraldine** (*tenderly*) You mustn't be sad for me, Alex. I'm happy. This is my life. After all I'm getting on for fifty now ——

**Alex** You're forty-one! Oh, my God, Gerry. I should never have left you. I wouldn't have let this happen to you.

**Geraldine** Nothing's happened to me. I've just found myself. The real me.

**Alex** No. You're absolutely wrong. You may think this is what you want but it isn't, it can't be! Even in those awful clothes you're still the most delectable woman in the world.

**Geraldine** (*very pleased*) I'm not.

**Alex** You are. So beautiful and sexy ... How Sidney could have believed him!

**Geraldine** Believed who? About what?

**Alex** Your ex. Telling her the marriage broke up because you were frigid.

**Geraldine** I was what!

**Alex** The full iceberg. He was so frustrated he was virtually driven by you into the arms of the Other Woman.

**Geraldine** Woman! There were at least half a dozen. What an absolute snake that man is. What a mean, low, sneaky ...

*Alex puts his arms around Geraldine*

Now, Alex.

**Alex** Tell me you still care about me.

**Geraldine** Well, of course I do, but I've put all that sort of thing behind me now.

**Alex** Never. Not you. God, it's so marvellous to hold you again. You can't go on leading this ludicrous, ridiculous life. I've come back and this time I am going to marry you.

**Geraldine** It's very sweet of you but ——

**Alex** Beautiful, adorable Gerry.

**Geraldine** (*helpless-ish*) Alex, don't. You mustn't.

**Alex** Shut up.

*Alex kisses Geraldine and, in spite of herself, she responds*

*The* UR *door opens and Sidney appears*

*Sidney watches Alex and Geraldine with a look of stunned surprise. They don't hear or see her. After a moment Sidney walks quietly over, stands behind them and gives them a slow handclap*

Mothering Sunday

**Sidney** Bravo!
**Geraldine** (*pushing Alex away*) How dare you? Let go of me!
**Alex** (*dazedly*) What?
**Sidney** (*cockney*) Oh, didn't you hear? She said "How dare you? Let go of me."
**Alex** Just a minute ——
**Geraldine** Be quiet, Alex. Now, Sidney, I don't want you to go thinking the wrong thing.
**Sidney** (*courteously; not cockney*) Don't you? Well perhaps you'd tell me the right thing to go thinking.

*Geraldine stares at her*

(*Cockney again*) I can still talk proper when I want to, you know. (*Not cockney*) It's quite clear that it was only my father you were frigid with.
**Geraldine** I have never been frigid!
**Alex** I'll drink to that.
**Geraldine** (*snapping*) I said be quiet!
**Sidney** Are you saying that my father lied to me?
**Geraldine** I certainly am.
**Sidney** But you were unfaithful to him with Alex.
**Geraldine** ⎫ (*together*) ⎧ No.
**Alex**     ⎭          ⎩ Yes.

*Geraldine glares at Alex*

**Geraldine** (*to Sidney*) The thing was that Alex had a foolish romantic crush on me in those days and when he saw me again this afternoon it all came back to him and I just felt sorry for him.
**Alex** Hang on. I ——
**Geraldine** (*overriding*) And as for your father, Sidney, I'm sorry to say that he is a man to whom fidelity does not come easily. If at all.
**Sidney** I don't want to hear about it!
**Alex** Oh listen, Sidney ——
**Sidney** Why should I listen? What good has it ever done me? This is what happens when you're an only child. Your parents are so

busy setting up rigged opinion polls about each other that there is seldom if ever any time left over to consider the actual feelings of the actual child. I think I should tell you that it is my definite intention to rearrange my life in such a way that I will never be obliged to see either you or my father ever again!

*Geraldine stares at Sidney*

**Geraldine** My God! Listen to you. (*Admiringly*) So articulate! Fantastic. Sidney, I insist that you reconsider about going to university. You're much too brilliant to throw away your life like this. And if your father won't pay for your tuition I'm sure you could get a scholarship or ——

**Alex** Gerry. She's at university.

**Geraldine** You are?

**Sidney** University College. And I've got a flat in Kensington. I only wear all this stuff with you.

**Geraldine** (*reproachfully*) Oh Sidney, a disguise? With your own mother? Doesn't that seem very ... (*she stops; then, quickly*) never mind, it doesn't matter now. This is such a relief. I can't tell you how happy I am.

**Alex** There's something I'd like to ——

**Geraldine** We must celebrate. There's no champagne but I've got some white wine in the fridge. (*She heads for the kitchen*) I'll just go and get it.

**Sidney** Mother! Were you listening to me? I have just finished saying that I don't want to see you or Dad ever again.

**Geraldine** Yes, but you didn't really mean it.

**Sidney** (*irritatedly*) How do you know?

**Geraldine** (*briskly*) Because I'm your mother.

*Sidney laughs in spite of herself. Geraldine laughs too*

**Alex** (*loudly*) Just a minute! May I say something?

**Geraldine** (*impatiently*) What is it, Alex?

**Alex** Don't you think it's time you told Sidney the truth too? And by the way, I've never slept with her.

Mothering Sunday                                                              19

**Sidney**  Who said you had?

**Alex**  I did.

**Sidney**  What a cheek!

**Alex**  You were the one that said we were living together.

**Geraldine**  I didn't really believe that.

**Sidney**  Yes, you did. You should've seen your face.

**Geraldine**  Oh, well, possibly just for a second I thought ——

**Alex**  I am trying to say something!

**Geraldine**  Sorry, Alex, do go on.

**Alex**  Sidney has a right to know that you and I are in love and we're going to get married.

**Sidney**  Is that true?

**Geraldine**  Of course it isn't. Honestly, Alex ——

**Alex**  No wait, Gerry. It's all right. I know Sidney will understand.

**Geraldine**  Understand what?

**Alex**  That you tried to turn yourself into a completely different person because you were feeling so lonely and unloved. You're leading this totally unreal life wearing those absurd clothes and surrounded by all this tat because you felt so rejected. First the divorce, then Sidney turning against you and, most important, me going away. Your father is wrong, Sidney. Gerry isn't basically dowdy ——

**Geraldine**  Dowdy!

**Alex**  What she is, is basically very insecure. I've only just realized it myself. For instance, I always thought she was bossy and domineering but now I see she only does all that to hide her real self. It's just self protection. But now ——

**Sidney**  Stop. (*To Geraldine*) You're really going to marry him?

**Geraldine**  Certainly not. I wouldn't dream of it.

**Alex**  (*moving to Geraldine*) Can't you see there's no need for pretence anymore?

**Geraldine**  I'm not pretending. (*She pats Alex*) Oh, Alex, no woman in her right mind would marry you.

**Alex**  You don't mean that. (*He is silent, mesmerized, during the following*)

**Geraldine**  Yes, I do. (*To Sidney*) He's very conceited, I'm afraid. And vain. Narcissistic, you could say.

**Sidney** Good-looking, though. And his clothes are nice.

**Geraldine** All part of the image. He spends a fortune on them. Not that he doesn't have some very nice qualities.

**Sidney** Yes. Good sense of humour. Really quite witty.

**Geraldine** And very intelligent. Terrifically high IQ. He's a brilliant writer.

**Sidney** Is he?

**Geraldine** Oh yes. But — (*regretfully*) He is a bother.

**Sidney** (*nodding*) I can see that, yes.

**Alex** (*"coming to"*) Right. That's it. Finish. I'm off.

**Geraldine** (*politely*) Must you go?

**Alex** (*snapping*) Yes I must. And I devoutly hope I will never see you again. You are without doubt a top-quality living example of exactly what drives men to chauvinism, drink and monasteries. (*To Sidney*) And as for you …

**Sidney** Don't worry about me. I can take the bus back.

**Alex** (*blinking*) Right. In that case, goodbye. (*He moves to the front door,* UR, *then turns back. Malevolently*) Ask her about the wrestler.

*Alex exits, slamming the door*

**Sidney** (*after a pause*) What did he mean?

**Geraldine** Nothing. Nothing at all. Just some preposterous fantasy.

*There is the sound of the car zooming off outside*

Well — he's gone. As they're always saying in Chekhov plays. Now, Sidney, you didn't really mean that about never seeing me again.

**Sidney** Yes. No. I don't know.

**Geraldine** Are you upset because Alex and I ——

**Sidney** Had a ding-dong?

**Geraldine** Oh really! Why does everybody call it that? An affair. We had an affair.

**Sidney** Whichever. No, I'm not upset about it, it's just things keep changing so fast. About this wrestler ——

# Mothering Sunday

**Geraldine** (*involuntarily*) Boxer. (*Quickly*) The fantasy. It was about a boxer.

**Sidney** A boxer and you.

**Geraldine** Well, yes. So stupid. Imagine. At my age!

**Sidney** You're not that old. And you're still quite attractive.

**Geraldine** Thanks very much.

**Sidney** No, I mean it. You are. As a matter of fact, I think it would be a good idea if you did have a boyfriend.

**Geraldine** You do?

**Sidney** It would bolster up your self-esteem for one thing.

**Geraldine** Ah.

**Sidney** But Alex was right about your clothes being a bit ludicrous.

**Geraldine** You think so?

**Sidney** Sorry. Yes. You've obviously taken refuge in a completely inappropriate self-image. It's a common form of denial. (*Beat*) Though in some ways it's quite nice to have a mother that actually looks like a mother. (*Not accusingly*) You never did.

**Geraldine** Sorry.

**Sidney** It's OK. I sort of liked it but the twinset and pearls are a mistake. You know, a lot of older women wear tracksuits nowadays.

**Geraldine** Perhaps I should try that.

**Sidney** Make sure you get a good one. (*Pause*) I could help you choose. If you'd like that.

**Geraldine** (*beaming*) Oh I would, I would.

**Sidney** Well, maybe we could go shopping together. And you could see my flat. Speaking of which, I don't like to sound rude — I can see you were aiming for the rustic look but I honestly think this room would work better very plain. Simple. Do you know what I mean?

**Geraldine** Ye … es, I think so.

**Sidney** Have I hurt your feelings?

**Geraldine** (*trying not to laugh*) No. Honestly not.

*In the distance the church clock strikes five*

**Sidney** Oh, the bus. It goes at twenty past.

**Geraldine** You never had any tea. Come into the kitchen and I'll get you a sandwich to take with you. I just didn't have time to bake a cake.
**Sidney** A sandwich will be fine.

*They exit* DR

*The door* UR *opens and Alex comes in warily. He listens at the door* DR *then moves to the sofa and hides behind it*

*There is a pause*

*Sidney and Geraldine enter* DR. *Sidney is carrying a plastic bag*

**Sidney** Thanks, this is great. (*She notices the knitting on the sofa*) I don't remember you ever knitting.
**Geraldine** Don't you? I was thinking of knitting you a cardigan.
**Sidney** Brilliant. Could it be cable?
**Geraldine** (*recklessly*) Why not?
**Sidney** Well … Goodbye — Mother.
**Geraldine** Goodbye, sweetheart. (*She takes Sidney's face in her hands and gives her a very loving kiss on the cheek*)

*Sidney and Geraldine smile at each other*

*Sidney exits. As she goes:*

**Sidney** I'll phone you.

*Geraldine follows Sidney off*

**Geraldine** (*off*) Yes, do. Goodbye. (*She calls*) Goodbye!

*Geraldine re-enters, kicks off her shoes, sinks on to the sofa and undoes the top button of her skirt*

God! So tight!

Mothering Sunday

*Doug appears* DR

**Geraldine** (*smiling lovingly*) Hallo.
**Alex** (*his head popping up from behind the sofa*) Hallo, Gerry.

*Gerry leaps up, very startled*

*Doug sees Alex and exits rapidly* DR

*Alex doesn't see Doug*

**Alex** (*smiling lovingly*) You knew I was here, didn't you? You could feel it.
**Geraldine** No. Yes. What? Why have you come back?
**Alex** Don't worry. Sidney didn't see me driving back. Do you know it took me all the way to the motorway turn-off before I suddenly realized why you'd lied?
**Geraldine** (*with a glance at the kitchen*) Lied? I don't know what you mean.
**Alex** About us. You and me. You were putting your daughter first. And I'm proud of you for that.
**Geraldine** (*lost*) Oh. Well. Thank you.
**Alex** You knew she wasn't ready yet for the idea of you getting married again. Forgive me for jumping the gun on that. You pretended to turn me down for her sake. Oh, Gerry, I could tell when you kissed me that you were still in love with me.

*Doug appears*

**Geraldine** Doug!
**Alex** Who the hell are you?
**Doug** (*promptly*) The plumber. Gerry, I ——
**Geraldine** Thank you, Douglas. There's no hurry about the washers. Come back tomorrow.
**Doug** (*unhappily*) I'd sooner stay and do it now, Gerry.
**Geraldine** Oh ... Well, all right. Carry on then.

*Geraldine pushes Doug into the kitchen and shuts the door*

**Alex** Where does he get off just walking in like that as if he owned the place? And calling you Gerry?

**Geraldine** We all call each other by first names in the village and country people always use the back door. He's just a local lad who does odd jobs and ——

*Alex moves towards Geraldine*

—— now Alex, please!

**Alex** I want to kiss you.

**Geraldine** Not now. He might come back.

**Alex** So what? I don't mind.

**Geraldine** I've got my reputation in the village to think about.

**Alex** Right. OK. That's fair. (*Buoyant*) Oh, Gerry, you're going to love Argentina.

*Doug enters*

**Doug** Argentina!

**Alex** (*startled*) My God! Yes, Argentina. What's it to you, plumber?

*Geraldine bundles Doug back towards the kitchen*

**Geraldine** Now, Douglas, please just ——

**Doug** (*resisting*) What's he talking about, Gerry? You're not going away, are you? Wanting to kiss you? What's going on? I thought he was Sidney's boyfriend. Who is he?

**Alex** Well! Well! Well! (*Pause*) I'll tell you who I am, Plumber. I'm the one who fell off the Christmas tree. And you must be Jojo.

**Doug** Eh?

**Geraldine** Alex, I don't know what you're thinking but ——

**Alex** What I'm thinking, Geraldine, is that they don't make gossip fast enough to keep up with you. The hottest tea cosy in town. Here he is, just like they said. The wrestler.

**Doug** Boxer.

**Alex** Well, you won't have to box me, Jojo. The prize is all yours.
**Doug** Why does he keep calling me Jojo?
**Geraldine** Oh, he's just being very stupid ——
**Alex** He certainly was. You can have her, you lucky fellow. For as long as you can stand it. But then I bet you love jumping through the hoops for the boss lady, don't you?
**Doug** Look, would you like your head punching?
**Alex** No thanks, Jojo, not today. Save your strength. You'll need it.

*Doug advances on Alex*

All right, all right, I'm going. For God's sake, Gerry, call him to heel or something.
**Geraldine** Douglas!

*Doug stops and turns back to Geraldine*

**Alex** Terrific, His Master's Voice. (*To Doug, confidingly*) Listen, mate, you could still escape — make a break for it like me. She'll eat you alive, believe me.

*Doug lunges at Alex*

Stay, Douglas, stay! I'm off. So long, Geraldine. Keep cracking the whip.

*Alex exits, slamming the door. There is a pause*

**Doug** He was your boyfriend then, Gerry?
**Geraldine** (*picking up cushions; impatiently*) Yes, yes. A long time ago.
**Doug** Were you in love with him?
**Geraldine** No! (*Pause*) Yes. (*Pause*) I can't remember. Help me with this stuff.
**Doug** (*not moving*) Were you going to go to Argentina with him?

**Geraldine** (*snapping*) No of course I wasn't. Stop nagging, Doug. (*She drops the cushions and starts to cry*)
**Doug** (*crushed*) You are in love with him.
**Geraldine** (*crying*) I am not. I'm in love with you.
**Doug** (*daring to hope*) You sure?
**Geraldine** (*still crying*) Yes!

*Doug goes to Geraldine and puts his arms around her*

**Doug** Then why are you crying? What is it, Gerry? What's wrong?
**Geraldine** (*looking up at Doug, in tears*) Do I crack the whip? Am I bossy and horrible and mean to you?
**Doug** (*amazed*) Course not!
**Geraldine** Tell me the truth, Doug. Do you think I'm like a sergeant-major?
**Doug** (*laughing*) Hey? You? What a daft thing to say. You're lovely, Gerry. You're just right.

*Geraldine finds a handkerchief and blows her nose. She smiles gratefully at Doug*

**Geraldine** Don't ever let me boss you, Doug. Promise me. Just don't let me. If I do, tell me to stop.
**Doug** Right. I will. I promise. (*He kisses Geraldine*)
**Geraldine** (*snuggling into him happily*) Do me a favour?

*Doug nods*

Go and get that bottle of white wine out of the fridge.

*Doug sets off for the kitchen*

And two glasses.
**Doug** (*stopping*) I can't have any, Gerry. I'm in training.
**Geraldine** Don't be silly. You can have one glass. We're celebrating.
**Doug** Celebrating what?
**Geraldine** You moving in.

**Doug** (*punching the air*) Yes!

*Doug exits into the kitchen*

*During the following, Geraldine puts things back into the chest, humming to herself*

*Doug comes back in with the wine bottle and two tumblers on a tray*

**Geraldine** Oh, honestly, not those glasses. Get the proper wine glasses.
**Doug** Sorry. (*He heads for the exit, then stops and clears his throat*) I think these ones are OK.
**Geraldine** (*the sergeant-major*) You what?
**Doug** (*putting down the tray; nervously*) I said I think these glasses are OK.

*Geraldine starts to speak, then stops. They look at each other. She moves towards him. He holds his ground. She starts to laugh*

**Geraldine** Yes, they are. They are OK. They're fine.

*Doug starts to laugh too. They move towards each other*

*The Lights fade to Black-out. Music*

# FURNITURE AND PROPERTY LIST

*On stage*: Low antique chest. *In it*: flowered cushions, antimacassars, big fringed satin shawl, lacy table runner, framed photographs, china ornaments, bright Spanish rug, painting of gaudy pastoral sunset scene, pair of bronzed baby shoes
Abstract painting
Modern sofa
Coffee table
Two good chairs
Bookshelf with books
Expensive oriental rug
Baby grand piano. *On it*: sheet music
Piano stool
Sports bag. *In it*: long scarf on knitting needles

*Off stage*: Plastic bag (**Sidney**)
Tray with two tumblers and a bottle of wine (**Doug**)

*Personal*: **Geraldine**: handkerchief

# LIGHTING PLOT

Practical fittings required; nil
Interior. The same throughout

*To open*: Darkness

| | | |
|---|---|---|
| *Cue* 1 | Piano music begins<br>*Bring up general interior lighting* | (Page 1) |
| *Cue* 2 | **Doug** leads **Geraldine** to the door UR<br>*Fade to black-out* | (Page 6) |
| *Cue* 3 | Car door opens and shuts<br>*Bring up general interior lighting* | (Page 6) |
| *Cue* 4 | **Doug** and **Geraldine** move towards each other<br>*Fade to black-out* | (Page 27) |

# EFFECTS PLOT

Effects marked * are applicable if the actors cannot play the piano and have to mime.

*Cue* 1  When ready  (Page 1)
*Music, cross-fading to * simple piece being played on piano, not very well*

*Cue* 2  * **Doug** hits a wrong note and stops playing  (Page 1)
*Cut music*

*Cue* 3  * **Doug** puts his hands on the wrong keys, plays, then stops  (Page 2)
*Burst of discordant music, suddenly stopping*

*Cue* 4  Lights fade to black-out  (Page 6)
*Music, cross-fading to distant sound of church bells striking three, sound of car pulling up outside with screeching brakes, car door opening and shutting*

*Cue* 5  * **Sidney** picks out the piece on the piano  (Page 10)
*One-finger rendition of simple piece*

*Cue* 6  * **Sidney** plays the piece all the way through  (Page 10)
*Good rendition of simple piece*

*Cue* 7  **Geraldine**: "Just some preposterous fantasy."  (Page 20)
*Car zooms off outside*

*Cue* 8  **Geraldine**: "No. Honestly not."  (Page 22)
*Distant sound of church bells striking five*

*Cue* 9  The Lights fade to Black-out  (Page 27)
*Music*

A licence issued by Samuel French Ltd to perform this play does not include permission to use the Incidental music specified in this copy. Where the place of performance is already licensed by the PERFORMING RIGHT SOCIETY a return of the music used must be made to them. If the place of performance is not so licensed then application should be made to the Performing Right Society, 29 Berners Street, London W1.

A separate and additional licence from PHONOGRAPHIC PERFORMANCES LTD, 1 Upper James Street, London W1R 3HG is needed whenever commercial recordings are used.